Matt
Groening

Other titles in the Inventors and Creators series include:

Inventors and Creators

Matt
Groening

Raymond H. Miller

KIDHAVEN PRESS
An imprint of Thomson Gale, a part of The Thomson Corporation

Detroit • New York • San Francisco • San Diego • New Haven, Conn. • Waterville, Maine • London • Munich

LIBRARY OF CONGRESS CATALOGING-IN-PUBLICATION DATA

Miller, Raymond H., 1967–
  Matt Groening / by Raymond H. Miller.
    p. cm. — (Inventors and creators)
  Includes bibliographical references and index.
  ISBN 0-7377-3158-3 (hard cover : alk. paper)
  1. Groening, Matt—Juvenile literature. 2. Cartoonists—United States—Biography—Juvenile literature. I. Title. II. Series.
  PN6727.G755Z7 2005
  741.5'092—dc22

                                                              2005012148

Contents

Chapter One

Born to Be Wild

Matthew Abram Groening was born on February 15, 1954, in Portland, Oregon, to Homer and Marge Groening. Matt was the third of five Groening children. He has an older brother named Mark, an older sister named Patty, and two younger sisters, Lisa and Maggie. The family's last name, which rhymes with *raining*, may have derived from Groningen, a city in the Netherlands. Homer Groening was born into a family of Mennonite farmers who had settled in Saskatchewan, Canada. He lived there as a child before moving to Oregon during his youth. He joined the U.S. military and fought in World War II, earning a Distinguished Flying Cross for his heroics in the historic D-day invasion of June 6, 1944.

When Homer Groening returned to Oregon after the war, he became a man of many talents. He started

Matt Groening, pictured with his cartoon creations, the Simpsons, was the third of five children born to Homer and Marge Groening.

an advertising agency in 1958 and produced his own commercials. He also directed and produced films and television shows. When he was not working at the office, he loved to doodle in his chair at home. Matt was fascinated with his father's cartoon drawings and soon showed an interest in learning how to draw his own. Homer brought home colored pencils and sketchpads for Matt and the other four children to use for practice. He would start a story and let the children finish it. Matt's cartoons were not very good at first, but Homer encouraged him to keep trying. He loved drawing pictures of Batman, Charlie Brown, Popeye, and others. Little by little, his sketches improved.

Exploring Portland

Matt grew up in Portland, a city known for its beautiful parks and scenic gorges, as well as a nuclear power plant and a polluted river. The Groening family lived on a winding, dead-end street named Northwest Evergreen Terrace in Portland's West Hills. Matt and his brothers and sisters often played with their friends from the neighborhood in the wooded hills surrounding their home. They sought adventures beyond those woods as well. The family lived between a new zoo and an old zoo, and each one was within walking distance from their home. The old zoo had closed in the late 1950s, and it became the perfect hangout for Matt and his friends. They ignored the No Trespassing signs and sneaked into the old zoo to play inside the abandoned cages. Matt even worked up the courage to take a swim in the stale green water of the bear pool.

Looking for Excitement

Matt risked getting into trouble at the new zoo as well. He used to hide behind the bushes near the tracks of the zoo's miniature train. As the train passed by, he would hop on board and ride the train for free. Earlier, when the train was being built, Matt and his brothers pushed one of the train's cars up the hill and rode it back down. When the car did not make the loop at the station and kept going, Matt panicked and jumped off. He rolled in the gravel, jumped to his feet, then found himself being chased by the police. Matt narrowly escaped, but the scare did not cause him to change his behavior. He and his friends went looking for more excitement, including watching movies for free. "We had ways of sneaking into the big downtown movie theaters," Matt recalled. "The Paramount and the Orpheum were the

As a boy, Matt often sneaked into Portland's movie theaters with his friends.

easy ones. We never could crack the Music Box. The Broadway was easy, too. We'd hide in the balcony of the Paramount and watch the ushers punch the curtains looking for kids sneaking in. It was quite dramatic."[1]

Problem Student

Matt continued his rebellious ways while attending Ainsworth Elementary in Portland. He was a gifted student who got good grades when he applied himself. But he rarely paid attention in class because he was too busy being bad. One of his favorite tricks was making high-pitched meowing sounds when the teacher's back was turned. When the teacher turned around, Matt sat quietly in his seat without cracking a smile and avoided

Matt was often punished by his teachers for misbehaving, like this boy forced to stand in a corner.

punishment. Once while playing in the playground, he screamed as loud as he could just for fun. A teacher nearby thought someone had a whistle and frantically searched for the guilty person. Again Matt kept a straight face. He and his friends laughed when the teacher finally gave up and angrily walked away.

Matt was not always so secretive while misbehaving in class. He often talked back to his teachers when they tried to correct him. He spent a great deal of time standing in the corner for his actions, but the punishment did little good. Once while standing in the corner, he made a hangman's noose out of string, which made the other students laugh. This only got him into more trouble with his teacher.

Matt's love of drawing also had a negative effect on his grades. He frequently sat in the back of the room and drew pictures at his desk. Once the teacher saw what he was doing, snuck up on him, and smacked his knuckles with a ruler. The teacher tore up the paper and gave Matt a lecture about paying attention in class. But it did little good. Matt was simply more interested in cartooning than focusing on his schoolwork. As a result, he did not learn how to multiply numbers between seven and thirteen—and still cannot to this day.

Going Underground

Because Matt loved drawing cartoons, he was naturally attracted to comic books. He spent hours at a time sitting inside a Portland comic book store reading *Fantastic Four, The Incredible Hulk,* and *The Amazing*

Spider-Man. But by the time he reached high school, he preferred underground comic books. These were darker, edgier, and more crudely drawn than popular comics. His favorite comics were *Zap*, by Robert Crumb, and Gilbert Shelton's *The Fabulous Furry Freak Brothers*. Many of the underground comic books were unpopular with parents and teachers, because many of them had rebellious themes and characters. This, of course, only caused Matt's interest in the underground scene to grow.

Turbulent Times

Matt attended Portland's Lincoln High in the late 1960s and early 1970s, which were very turbulent times. Like the rest of the nation, Lincoln High was divided over the Vietnam War. Protests against the war took place often at the school, and Matt was a frequent participant. But most of his time was spent on much lighter issues. He wrote stories, drew cartoons, and made films with friends who shared his love for creativity. One of the films they produced was called *Lightning Tour of Lincoln*, a minute-long race through the halls of Lincoln High. Matt also helped to develop a student political group called Teens for Decency. The group created a sarcastic campaign for the school elections and promoted their cause with the slogan "If you're against decency, what are you for?"[2] It was meant to be a joke, but the other students liked it so much they elected Matt student body president.

Matt also found time to contribute articles and cartoons to the school newspaper, and he helped to organize the Komix Appreciation Club. It was a club for students

As an adolescent, Matt was fascinated by underground comic-book artists like Robert Crumb.

who shared his appreciation for underground comic books. The group eventually began publishing its own underground newspaper, called *Bilge Rat*. The newspaper featured a cartoon character named Ace Noodleman that Matt created. He drew Noodleman and most of his other cartoons the same way. The characters had bulging eyes and severe overbites. Matt was developing his own style that he hoped someday might lead to a career in drawing.

Chapter Two

Life in Los Angeles

Matt graduated from Lincoln High in 1972, then turned his attention to college. He wanted to go to Harvard but his application was turned down. His other choice was Evergreen State College in Olympia, Washington, which accepted him. He was interested in Evergreen because it was a new, experimental school and radically different from other colleges. Students were not given tests or grades, nor did they take regular classes. Instead they attended seminars. This all fit in with Matt's belief that grades were unfair and that traditional school structure was designed to control students. He later explained, saying, "It seems the main rule that traditional schools teach us is how to sit in rows quietly, which is perfect training for grown-up work in a dull office or factory, but not so good for education."[3]

The relaxed atmosphere at Evergreen left Matt time to practice his drawing. But he did not like how his cartoons were turning out. He began to believe

After high school, Matt Groening attended Washington's experimental Evergreen State College.

that he would never be good enough to draw professionally and that cartooning would probably have to remain a hobby. Matt loved to write, however, and was considering a career in journalism. He spent much of his time at Evergreen working at the college newspaper, the *Cooper Point Journal*. He was the editor of the paper and worked alongside his friend and fellow Evergreen student Lynda Barry. An amateur cartoonist herself, Barry's style was not as dark or serious as that of other underground cartoonists. Her cartoons were funnier and more personal than any Matt had seen. Barry, who later went on to a successful career as a cartoonist, became an influence on Matt. His work gradually became lighter and funnier than it had ever been. Still, cartooning remained just a hobby. His first choice in careers after college was in journalism.

Job Search

When Matt graduated from Evergreen State College in the spring of 1977, he applied for a reporting job back in Portland at his hometown newspaper, the *Oregonian*. He was turned down, however, because the editor there was

As a student at Evergreen State College (pictured), Matt worked as an editor for the campus newspaper and he even considered a career in journalism.

not happy with Matt's direction of the *Cooper Point Journal*. The editor thought the underground style and attitude Matt had instilled at the college newspaper was a disgrace. The recent college graduate was told he would never get a journalism job in the Pacific Northwest. Matt did not take the words to heart, but even so, he decided to search elsewhere. That summer he packed his bags and headed for southern California.

Matt chose Los Angeles because he had heard that writers in the city were paid well for their work and that jobs were plentiful. His career did not get off to a promising start, however. As soon as he got to Los Angeles, his rusty old car broke down, leaving him stranded in the middle of the freeway in extreme heat. Matt's luck did not improve any time soon. He had very little money and could barely afford the rent for a tiny upstairs apartment. During the day, he traveled around Los Angeles looking for a job. At night, he returned to his cramped apartment and worked on his cartoons. Matt had a hard time concentrating though, because a man in the apartment below played his stereo with the volume turned all the way up. Matt yelled, stomped his feet, and even tried blasting his own stereo to make the man turn down the music, but nothing worked. Only when Matt dropped a cinder block on his floor did the man below get the message.

Ghostwriter

During his first several weeks in Los Angeles, Matt had no luck finding work. Then, while looking through the classified advertisements section of the *Los Angeles Times*, he came across a job listing for a "writer/chauffeur." He thought the job sounded interesting and decided to apply. Matt received an interview and was hired. Finally, Matt had his first writing job, but it was not what he had hoped. His main responsibility was driving an 88-year-old movie director around Los Angeles to his various appointments during the day. At night, Matt became a ghostwriter. He sat at a desk, recalled stories the old director had told about himself earlier that day, and wrote the man's autobiography. Matt hated the job and later

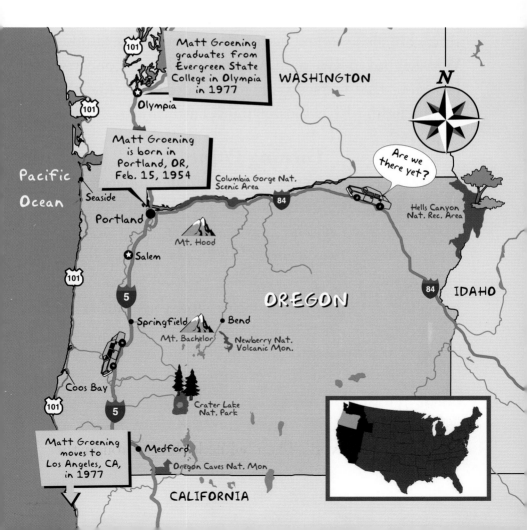

explained why he eventually quit. "His manuscript was already over a thousand pages; previous writer/chauffeurs had already been working on [it]. Unfortunately, the book was totally obsessed with the director's mother; he'd lived with her until she was 105 years old. And every single part of the book was about her."[4]

Matt took on some odd jobs to earn money. He worked for a short time at a sewage treatment plant as a landscaper. One of Matt's passions was music, and he was hired as a clerk at a record store on Sunset Boulevard called Licorice Pizza. Among other responsibilities, he gave away free licorice to customers of the store. He also worked across the street at the famous Whiskey a Go-Go, a club that hosted rock concerts. He came face to face with rock-and-roll stars of the day, including Elvis Costello and Patti Smith.

Turning Point

In 1977, Matt began producing a simple underground comic strip about life in Los Angeles. He called it *Life in Hell.* In the cartoon, Matt expressed the fears and frustrations he was feeling. But he did it in a lighthearted way. The comic strip was based on a lonely but extremely bitter cartoon rabbit named Binky. Matt photocopied a series of cartoons, stapled them into a booklet, and mailed them to his friends back in Portland. They thought the cartoons were hilarious and urged him to send more.

Matt was thrilled to hear they loved his work and wondered if others would be interested in it. About

After he moved to Los Angeles, Matt worked several odd jobs, including one at the city's famous Whiskey a Go-Go club.

that time, punk rock was becoming popular, and Licorice Pizza devoted a small section of the store to selling punk records and magazines. Matt put some copies of his underground book on a shelf to see how well they would sell. Some of the punk fans stole the comic and tore it up because they hated it. Others loved it and became devoted fans. Amazingly, Matt was soon making 500 copies to keep up with demand.

Matt showed his work to the editor of an alternative weekly newspaper called the *Los Angeles Reader* in hopes of getting a job. The editor was impressed and offered Matt a job on the spot. But the young writer was disappointed when he found out he was being hired to work in the circulation department, not to produce his cartoons. He needed a full-time job, however, and accepted.

In 1978, Matt's *Life in Hell* began appearing in *Wet,* a contemporary magazine with articles related to water

In 1978 Matt's *Life in Hell* cartoon began appearing in *Wet,* a magazine with few readers.

and bathing. The cartoon was mostly text, and the magazine had few subscribers. But Matt was just happy being published, and it gave him hope that it might lead to better opportunities. Meanwhile, he worked his way up at the *Reader*. He was promoted to typesetting and pasting up copy, then eventually he began editing articles. In 1980, three years after setting out in his old car for Los Angeles, his hard work finally paid off. The editor of the *Reader* offered Matt space in the newspaper for his *Life in Hell* cartoon. The young cartoonist happily accepted.

Chapter Three

The Simpsons

Groening ended up doing more at the *Los Angeles Reader* than just producing his *Life in Hell* comic strip. He finally attained his goal of becoming a journalist when he started contributing articles about rock and roll as a music critic. For some of his articles, he got to interview popular musicians. He once met with David Byrne, lead singer of the Talking Heads, for an article he was writing about the successful 1980s band.

Meanwhile, *Life in Hell* was gaining fans because of Matt's clever wit. He created new characters to complement Binky. They included Sheba, Binky's girlfriend, and Bongo, Binky's five-year-old son from a previous relationship. Bongo had one ear and was just as nervous and insecure as his father. Groening also added Jeff and Akbar, two characters who appeared to be twin brothers. They were perfectly matched in short pants, fez hats with tassels, and Charlie Brown-style striped shirts. Jeff and Akbar were entrepreneurs who opened several businesses, including a shop in a strip mall called Tofu Hut.

Matt Groening began winning new fans after *Life in Hell* appeared in the *Los Angeles Reader* for the first time in 1980.

By 1986, *Life in Hell* had become such a sensation with readers that Groening decided to publish a book of cartoons called *Work is Hell*. It was a humorous book about life in the workplace featuring Bongo and several other *Life in Hell* characters. As usual, Matt parodied, or made fun of, bosses and other authority figures. While out of town promoting his new book, Groening learned that the *Reader* was canceling his comic strip and that he was being fired from his rock critic position at the newspaper. He was told the decision to let him go was the result of him complaining about a fellow staff writer being fired. He took the rejection in stride, though. By that time, Groening's cartoon was being published in several magazines and newspapers across the country.

Hitting It Big

Groening soon went to work as a writer for another alternative newspaper called the *L.A. Weekly*. There, he met a woman named Deborah Caplan. The two formed a close relationship and started a business called ACME Features, under which they distributed Groening's comic strip. In 1987, the coworkers married and later had two children, sons Homer and Abe. They eventually formed Life in Hell Inc., and Deborah became Matt's manager. Under her direction, the company began producing merchandise, including calendars, coffee cups, and T-shirts featuring Matt's cartoon characters. She even arranged several book deals for Matt. But his work was about to enter the ultimate medium of television.

Groening's sharp-witted cartoon caught the attention of James L. Brooks, a successful television and movie producer and director. Brooks had been hired by the new FOX Broadcasting Company to produce *The Tracy Ullman Show,* a comedy variety show starring the popular British comedian. It was Brooks's idea to

In the late 1980s, producer James L. Brooks (pictured) offered Groening a chance to animate cartoon shorts for television.

use brief cartoon clips, called animated shorts, between skits on the show. He thought an animated version of the *Life in Hell* comic strip would be ideal.

Just before Groening went into the meeting with Brooks and FOX representatives, he created an entirely new set of cartoon characters in his mind. Groening described why: "I knew this was a big chance. And I was going to do the 'Life in Hell' characters but then I thought, Hmm, I'd never really done animation before. If I did animation and it was crummy, then maybe it would taint the comic strip—which was doing just fine. So that's why I made up the Simpsons."[5]

Before meeting with Brooks and FOX representatives, Groening created a new set of cartoon characters that he named the Simpsons.

A Boy Named Bart

FOX executives loved the idea and wanted Groening, thirty-two years old at the time, to create his cartoon for the show. Groening immediately went to work developing *The Simpsons,* a dysfunctional, or abnormal, family that lived in the fictional town of Springfield. The show featured Homer, the hilarious but crude father; Marge, a loving mother with a large blue beehivelike hairdo; their genius daughter Lisa; and Maggie, their pacifier-sucking baby. Groening named these four characters after his own parents and younger sisters. But the real star of the show—Homer and Marge's ten-year-old son, Bart—was based on a younger version of himself. Originally, Bart's name was even going to be Matt, but he thought the connection was too close to real life. He instead settled on a name that closely resembled the word "brat."

When *The Simpsons* debuted on *The Tracy Ullman Show* in the spring of 1987, fans of Groening's work instantly recognized a comical resemblance between Homer and Bart and the gang and the *Life in Hell* characters. "Over the years I've developed a style that's very simple," Groening said. "The problem is taking that style and trying to develop a variety of individuals. The temptation is to pile on detail."[6] To avoid that problem, he made the faces of the Simpson family members similar to one another. For simplicity, they all displayed the distinctive overbite that had long been a Groening design trait. Their skin was yellow and they had big, bulging eyes.

People loved the look of *The Simpsons,* but it was the sound of the show that made it complete. Bart Simpson's voice did not come from a boy, but was instead contributed by a female actor named Nancy Cartwright. She gave Bart the perfect squeaky voice the character needed to match his bratty appearance.

Groening's animated shorts gained a loyal following. *The Simpsons* made appearances in 50 episodes in the show's first three seasons. When the variety show was canceled after the fourth season on the air, FOX executives knew they had a potential hit in *The Simpsons*. They decided to give Groening his own show, because the young network desperately needed a hit to compete against television's so-called Big Three: ABC, CBS, and NBC.

Successful Start

Groening became an executive producer of the show and agreed to make thirteen half-hour episodes for the 1989–1990 television season. Partnering with Brooks and Sam Simon, another executive producer, Groening assembled a team of comedy writers and began creating the episodes. The first official show aired a week before Christmas in 1989. It was called "The Simpsons Christmas Special: Simpsons Roasting on an Open Fire." In the show, Christmas was nearly ruined for the Simpsons when Bart came home with a tattoo. Marge was horrified and spent all of the family's gift money to remove the tattoo. Homer then went to work as a department store Santa to pay for gifts. But he gambled away all of his earnings at the dog track when he bet on a losing greyhound named

Groening's animated shorts first aired in 1987 during a television variety show that starred Tracy Ullman.

Santa's Little Helper. The episode ended happily when Homer and Bart adopted the losing dog and brought it home for Christmas. Television viewers had never seen anything quite like *The Simpsons,* and the show created a buzz that began to sweep the nation.

In the episodes that followed, Groening and the writers rewarded curious viewers by adding to their cast of oddball characters, including Grandpa, Mr. Burns,

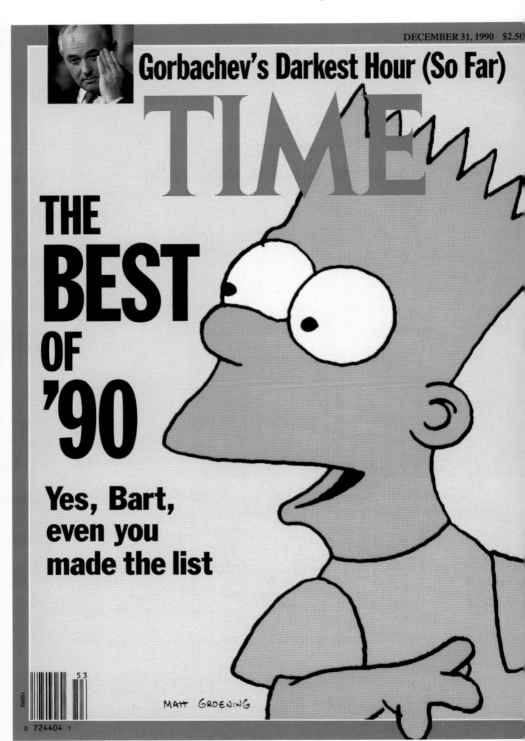

As one of the most important figures of 1990, Bart Simpson dominates the cover of the year-end issue of *Time* magazine.

Smithers, Principal Skinner, and Ned Flanders. Many aspects of the show closely resembled Groening's early life in Portland—from Springfield's nuclear power plant, where Homer works as a safety inspector, to the location of the family's home on Evergreen Terrace.

Critics loved the show for its wit, and *The Simpsons* quickly became a television sensation. It won an Emmy Award in the category of Outstanding Animated Program after its first season. FOX executives were thrilled with the success of the show. Groening was just happy to be able to present his comical and twisted view of the world to such a large audience.

Chapter Four

Futurama and Beyond

In the early 1990s, *The Simpsons* became an American pop-culture phenomenon. Words or phrases from the show started popping up in everyday conversations, such as Homer's "Doh!" and Bart's "Don't have a cow, man!" Merchandise featuring Bart and the gang was also very popular among children as well as adults. *The Simpsons* T-shirts, video games, watches, and lunch boxes could be found in nearly every arcade, school, and shopping mall in America.

But not everyone was a fan of the show. Bart's tendency to mock teachers, disobey his parents, and occasionally use foul language created a backlash. Some people thought the show was offensive and potentially harmful to the American family. They were comforted when President George H.W. Bush said at the 1992 conference of National Religious Broadcasters, "We need a nation closer to the Waltons than the Simpsons."[7] He was referring to the 1970s television drama

The Waltons, which portrayed a poor but close-knit family living in the Great Depression of the 1930s and early 1940s. The Walton children respected their parents, and the show generally had a wholesome quality.

President Bush's plea seemed to backfire when *The Simpsons* became one of the most watched shows on television. Millions of fans tuned in each week to see what hilarious high jinks Homer and his family had in store. Adding to the show's humor was Groening's frequent use of popular guest stars, who seemed eager to lend their voices to "Simpsonized" versions of themselves. Stars ranging from legendary actress Elizabeth Taylor to the Rolling Stones' Mick Jagger made guest appearances on the show.

In the 1990s, *The Simpsons* became a merchandising sensation, with everything from dolls to video games for sale.

Over the years, Groening has received numerous awards and recognition for *The Simpsons*.

The awards kept coming for Groening's creation. *The Simpsons* was nominated for an amazing seven more Emmys during the 1990s, winning four times.

A New Project

As the decade of the 1990s neared an end, Groening's role on *The Simpsons* was evolving. As executive producer, he was leaving the daily task of writing new episodes up to his team of writers. He still oversaw the creative direction of the show, however, and the writers often turned to him for suggestions. Leaving the writing to others gave Groening time to devote to his *Life in Hell* cartoon, which he had continued to write even when he was working on *The Simpsons*. "I'll never give up the comic strip," he once said. "It's my foundation."[8]

Despite the success of his television show and comic strip, Groening was ready for something new. He was a

Although *The Simpsons* is created by a team of writers and artists, Groening continues to oversee the creative direction of the show.

longtime fan of science fiction and was interested in developing an animated sitcom about the future. He began planning a show that blended the attitude of *Life in Hell* with the look of *The Simpsons*. He eventually called it *Futurama*. He presented the idea to FOX on the condition that he be allowed to have complete creative control over the show. This was partly because he wanted to prove he could produce a successful show on his own. The network was eager for another hit from Groening and signed him on for thirteen episodes.

Futurama was centered around a character named Fry, a pizza-delivery man who was accidentally frozen in a high-tech laboratory. Defrosted 1,000 years later, he went to work for an intergalactic delivery service. Fry worked alongside Leela, the one-eyed captain of the spaceship, and Bender, a disgruntled and crude robot. To the delight of fans of *The Simpsons*, the cartoon characters were drawn in the same simple style as those on Groening's hit show. They displayed the same bulging eyes and exaggerated overbites.

Personal and Professional Disappointment

Shortly after FOX and Groening came to an agreement on *Futurama*, network executives began to have doubts about the series. They worried that Groening's show was too dark and negative for many television viewers. The network refused to give Groening total creative control over *Futurama* and made certain demands to make the show lighter and funnier.

Groening was angry about the creative restrictions forced on him by FOX. He described the process of getting *Futurama* on the air as the worst experience of his adult life. Making matters worse was the fact that Groening's marriage of fourteen years to Deborah Caplan was failing. The two later filed for divorce.

Futurama finally made it on the air, debuting in the spring of 1999. It appeared on a Sunday night between episodes of *The Simpsons* and *X-Files,* two of FOX's most popular shows. Watched by an amazing 19 million viewers, it appeared that Groening had another

Groening drew the characters of *Futurama* with the same simple style as *The Simpsons.*

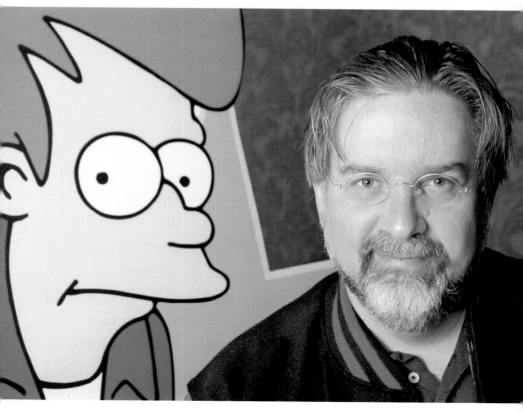

hit on his hands. But then the network moved the show to Tuesday night, and the audience fell to about 8 million viewers. The move angered Groening. Despite the friction between Groening and FOX executives, the show ran for four years and built a steady and devoted audience. In one of the show's funnier moments, viewers catch a glimpse of *The Simpsons* on television.

Eventually FOX canceled the series because of low ratings. The last episode appeared in August 2003.

Still Going Strong

Today, Groening continues to create his weekly cartoon, *Life in Hell*. It currently appears in about 250 newspapers. He also keeps busy as the owner and publisher of Bongo Comic Group, which he started in 1993. The group produces merchandise for all of Groening's work. It publishes several comics relating to *The Simpsons,* including Bart's favorite comic book on the show, *Radioactive Man.*

In addition to his weekly cartoon, comic publishing, and television producing responsibilities, Groening plays in a celebrity band with other writers. They are called the Rock Bottom Remainders. The name is a publishing term for books that do not sell.

Groening has gone from simple underground comic writer to the creator of a cartoon empire. *The Simpsons* is shown in more than 60 countries. The franchise, which includes reruns, books, calendars, toys, and even breakfast foods, is worth about $1 bil-

Together with authors Stephen King and Amy Tan (shown performing), Groening is part of a celebrity rock band known as the Rock Bottom Remainders.

lion. It continues to do well in the ratings and shows no signs of slowing down. The 2004–2005 season marks its sixteenth season on the air, the longest run for any television sitcom in history.

As for the future, Groening wants to continue working on *The Simpsons* as long as fans of the show

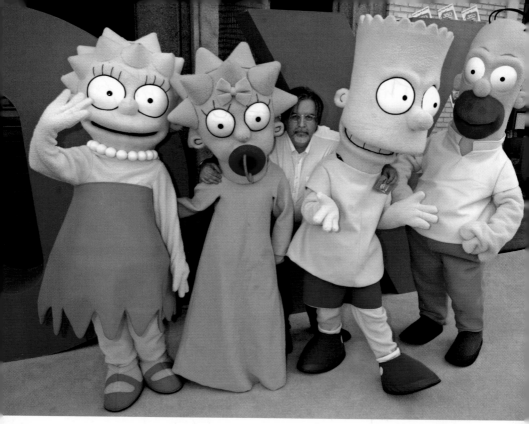

Matt Groening plans to continue working on *The Simpsons* as long as fans are thoroughly entertained by the show.

find it fresh and funny. He also plans on continuing his *Life in Hell* comic strip and may even try to get another groundbreaking television show on the air. Eventually, however, Groening plans to leave the hectic celebrity lifestyle of Los Angeles and return to his hometown. "I'm just temporarily relocated," he says of his nearly 30 years of living in Los Angeles. "I'm moving back. I love Portland."[9]

Notes

Chapter One: Born to Be Wild

1. Quoted in Don Hamilton, "Matt Groening's Portland," *Portland Tribune,* July 19, 2002.
2. Quoted in Hamilton, "Matt Groening's Portland."

Chapter Two: Life in Los Angeles

3. Quoted in Jim Carlile, "Matt Groening . . . Almost Caught on Tape," *Olympian,* May 28, 2000.
4. Quoted in Richard von Busack, "'Life' Before Homer," *Metro Active Arts,* November 2, 2000.

Chapter Three: *The Simpsons*

5. Quoted in Jay Babcock, "Meet the Maker: Matt Groening Interview." http://JayBabcock.com/Groening.html.
6. Quoted in Erik H. Bergman, "Prime Time Is Heaven for 'Life in Hell' Artist," *TV Host,* December 16, 1989.

Chapter Four: *Futurama* and Beyond

7. Quoted in Steve Hockensmith, "Simpsons Family Values," *Book,* November/December 2001.
8. Quoted in Bergman, "Prime Time Is Heaven for 'Life in Hell' Artist."
9. Quoted in Hamilton, "Matt Groening's Portland."

For Further Exploration

Books

Matt Groening, *Cartooning with the Simpsons.* New York: Perennial Currents, 1993. *The Simpsons* creator shows readers how to draw Bart, Homer, and the rest of the family in easy step-by-step directions.

————, *Futurama Adventures.* New York: Perennial Currents, 2004. A compilation of five comic books featuring Groening's most recent animated series.

————, *The Simpsons: A Complete Guide to Our Favorite Family.* New York: Perennial Currents, 1997. An in-depth look at *The Simpsons'* first ten years on television. Includes a description of each episode in the order it appeared.

————, *The Simpsons Guide to Springfield.* New York: Perennial Currents, 1998. A humorous guide to the fictional hometown of Homer, Marge, Bart, and the rest of the Simpsons.

Web Sites

Matt Groening's Portland (www.portlandtribune. com/simpsons). A clickable map of Portland that describes places of importance during Groening's youth.

TheSimpsons.com (www.thesimpsons.com). The official Web site of *The Simpsons.* Includes news, character profiles, episode guides, and information about future episodes.

Index

Picture Credits

Cover: © Richard Melloul/SYGMA/CORBIS
AFP/Getty Images, 13 (bottom)
© Bureau L.A. Collection/CORBIS, 26
© Dave G. Houser/CORBIS, 21
© Douglas Kirkland/CORBIS, 28, 37
Fred Prouser/Reuters/Landov, 42
© G.E. Kidder Smith/CORBIS, 17
Getty Images, 13 (top), 25
© John McAnulty/CORBIS, 9
Maury Aaseng, 19
© MC Leod Murdo/CORBIS SYGMA, 39
© O'Neill Terry/CORBIS SYGMA, 31
Patrick Harbron/Landov, 16, 22
© Reuters/CORBIS, 36
© Richard Melloul/SYGMA/CORBIS, 7, 35
© Roy Morsch/CORBIS, 10
© Steve Sands/CORBIS, 41
Time-Life Pictures/Getty Images, 32

About the Author

Raymond H. Miller is the author of more than fifty nonfiction books for children. He has written on a range of topics from U.S. presidents to Native Americans. He enjoys playing sports and spending time outdoors with his wife and two daughters.